The Love Triangle

The Love Triangle

Amor Amii

To order additional copies of this book, contact:
Xlibris
844-714-8691
www.Xlibris.com
Orders@Xlibris.com
829735

Contents

Acknowledgments

I want to thank my family for their support and for encouraging me to tell my story. I want to also thank my friend Shirley for helping me get this book together. I have been so exhausted with anxiety and busy with other things that it has taken me thirty years to complete it.

Amor

Reason for writing this book: I wrote this book to make the reader aware of the deception of others.

I want them to know how people will take advantage of your good nature and kindness. Looks are not everything. It is more of what's on the inside as opposed to what's on the outside. Choose a person who shows respect and care.

Preview: The author will take you from laughter, disappointments, discouragements, disloyalty, and back to love and excitement.

At first I thought my husband was a real Tony Curtis and I was so blessed to have him in my life.

However, shortly after we were married, he began dating every woman he could find and acted as if he had no time for me. Yet he refused to leave me or let me leave him. He said if I left him, he would lay in the woods, and even if it took months, he would kill my whole family.

Introduction

Caught up in a world of love, betrayal, and deception, I found love on a three-way street; love was gained after hate, betrayal, and deception almost destroyed me.

You know one never knows or suspects what will happen during their lifetime, or maybe I should say what type of life one will be living. As for me, I had a rocky beginning because my first marriage was scary and unbelievable. My second marriage left me mystified. My third marriage was totally loving from beginning to end, and we lived happily ever after. Therefore, I decided to write about them. Maybe this true story will be some insight for someone else out there who reads it.

God in heaven only knows what will happen with the

individual. Also, I believe that it is through no fault of the individual that things happen to them. The old saying "You reap what you sow" means what it says to some people, but in some cases, people reap a lot in which they haven't sown. Take for instance in my life, I tried almost always to be obedient to my parents and help others and live by the rules. I always tried to have empathy for others and love my enemy and neighbor. Living by the golden rule and treating everybody right has been a part of me. I feel that my reaping was totally different.

Personally, I think that I just haphazardly came across some bad situations in my life due to not knowing or not being told how some people's culture differs and just exactly what to expect out of life. Being a country girl not being able to travel to different places and meet different people while growing up have had some bearing on my situation. Also, my mom and daddy never traveled a lot, so really, how could they tell me what to expect? They hadn't experienced a lot either.

One could say that I was naive, and they would be right. I was too trusting and too forgiving, and the people I came into contact with saw it and took advantage of my good nature. The sad part of this is that I did not know the extent of my being sheltered or how vulnerable I was. I thought I had all the answers and could easily get what I wanted. I had some education, and I could sing and had a good raising with aspects of respect and consideration for others. At the same time, I was very shapely and had confidence in myself and my abilities to attract friends. As I got older, I have learned that everything is not meant for everybody—what's for you may not be for me. That's wisdom.

My Early Life

Sometimes after school, I would go to my aunt and uncle's house; they were like my second parents. My uncle was my dad's brother, and my aunt was my mom's sister. They never had any children. One day I was playing around with their hen and her chicks. I was trying to pick one up. She started coming after me, and as I was running, she caught my clothing with her beak and was clinging on to me. Whoa, I knew that would have been a nice YouTube video. You should have seen me running and screaming; she finally turned loose, and I guess she got tired.

We didn't have TV in the home and no form of communication except for radio, social meetings, and just simply word of mouth. I grew up in a small furniture-making town, where there were more large families than small ones. My family consisted of sixteen people, all total twelve girls and four boys, which included three sets of twins, one of which was me. My mama always told me that because I was a twin, I had gained my brother's share of life's problems, and because I was good to other people, God would bless me for life. Why she told me this is because my twin brother was stillborn. My father was a furniture worker, and my mother did domestic work. Mother was having children one every two years. One wonders just how hard life was trying to care for and feed us all. My mother was one tough cookie and a very loving person along with my father. I remember that I would wake up early in the morning, my mom would be making breakfast for my Dad, who would leave very early to catch his ride to work. His ride was a bus my mom's cousin drove to carry workers to start their day. Meanwhile, my dad would be holding my youngest twin sisters and trying to comfort them with their bottles, one on each knee, until my mom finished the breakfast and packed his lunch. Because he didn't drive, he would walk about a mile in the cold, the rain, and the snow. I often wondered how my dad kept shiny shoes and managed not to step in the mud. The roads back then were not paved.

Being that I grew up in a large family, I learned a lot. Most of all, I learned how to appreciate what I had and how hard it was to get. As kids, we use to play with rag dolls, which we sometimes made from old socks and yarn. We made playhouses in the woods by sweeping a space we would call our house and then surrounding the certain area with sticks from trees to separate my house from my sisters or brothers. We sang songs and pretended that we were having a funeral; we would dig a hole and use a stump for the body and sang "He died in 19——," acting sad and crying. As children, we played innocently and made up games to amuse ourselves. My brother and I would play with wagon wheels. We would put a stick in the center and roll them one hand on each side with our buttock in the air. I got hurt when my wheel hit a rock and the stick hit me in the eye. The next day, my eye was swollen up really, really large. My mom took care of it the best she could. All my siblings laughed at me and called me Cow's Eye. To this day, I still have sand in my eye and the scar, since we didn't have money to see a doctor unless it was a major issue. Also, our Christmas items were at my aunt and uncle's house. We would be all excited to wake up and walk in the cold about a half a mile to see what Santa brought. One toy each and a brown bag of goodies, nothing made us happier.

We never had air-conditioning or inside toilets during our younger life. There were regular fans sometimes, and there were buckets to be used at night (called slop jars). During the day, we had to use the outside toilet, or johnnie houses. Sometimes there would be big spiders and snakes inside, and you would have to be careful not to sit on the toilet seat without looking carefully. Another thing was the washing of clothes; we had a washing machine called a ringer washer. You would wash the clothes and then run them through the ringer at the top so the clothes could be squeezed between two rolling pins and the water pressed out. Then there was no such thing as an inside dryer. The dryer was the outside clothesline. (This was the best thing any way, and I think the most economical.) We had to use lamplight to see. By the way, our water was caught in barrels from the rain, or our dad and uncle would haul it in barrels from the spring or creek. Our drinking water was carried in buckets from the spring. The spring was some distance from the house, and so we carried the water. My dad kept the spring cleaned out. I remember this one time, my grandfather went to clean the spring out. My mother begged him not to go because he had gotten old and didn't have good mobility. Her words were "Papa. You don't need to go." He went anyway. Several hours passed, and we realized that he still hadn't returned. My brother and I went looking for him, and to our surprise, he was straddled in the spring and could not get up, one leg on one side and vice versa, with his head on the big rock at the top of the spring. We had to pull him up so he could stand. Poor grandpa. I felt like crying to actually see him this way, not able to get himself up. My final memory of Grandpa was when he would make homemade wine from pork salad berries and dandelions. They say they are poisonous, but it didn't bother him. Not at all.

Our clothes were made by us or someone would give them to us, hand-me-down clothing. When we made our own, we used old feed sacks that the hogs or cows feed came in. Also, fabric was twenty to fifty cents per yard then. My shoes were also hand-me-downs (smile); my feet are still bad today. I cherished those shoes; they were cute ones. Sometimes the shoes were not quite big enough, but that was the best my parents could afford. I remember one time my shoes got wet and I needed them to wear to school the next day, so I put them into the oven to dry. I forgot I had put them in, and they shrunk to a smaller size. They also turned up at the toes, as if they were looking at me. I was unable to wear them the next day. I don't quite remember what I wore, but I did go to school the next day.

I started out going to a one-room school. It was a log cabin one. Despite adverse condition, we had lots of fun. The teacher would call each grade, one at a time, for different classes from 1 to 6. All this in one room. I remember that I would finish first, and then I was called on to help some of the other students who were unable to understand the assignment.

During this time, discipline was administered using switches from the outside trees. One student was sent to get the switch from the woods or the teacher used a bat with holes in it. When the teacher would hit your buttocks, the bat would suck your skin up in the holes a little, a painful experience. Also, I remember the teacher making one girl stand on one leg and foot for several hours. I distinctly remember one boy whom the teacher would send to the spring to bring the water, and we wondered why the water had a peculiar taste. The boy had urinated in it. Boy, did he get it. He got a whipping that I don't think he will never forget. He was just the type of person who had to be disciplined all the time. I heard that his grandmother would beat him all the time, so maybe he needed psychological help. During this time, no one heard or knew what this kind of help was. When the teacher would whip him, he would dance all around as if he was popping corn. We would laugh a little and try to cover our mouths so he wouldn't see us. I lived close to my school, so my aunt would get on the horse named Bob, put me up when it would rain, and we would carry lunch to my other siblings.

Later, after attending the one-room school for about three years, another modern school was built. Then we had to ride the bus to school. Before then, I never knew what this was like because my first school was close by home and I could walk. While attending school at the new school from grades 3 to 7, I joined the Glee Cub, 4-H, modeling, and other extracurricular activities. We used to have May Day. This is when we would have our little crepe paper dresses and would wrap the May Pole. Boy, I would be so happy; I loved it.

At the end of the day and in the morning, while riding the school bus, several other students would always harass us and call us names and ridicule us for no apparent reason.

I would guess it was jealousy. This was pure harassment and what one would call bullying today. My dad was harassed at work also. He said that this man he knew would sneak into his lunch and place hot sauce into his sandwiches. We would wear nice clothes to school even though we had sixteen in our family and one parent working. We managed to wear these nice clothes because we made them ourselves and because my aunt and sister sent us nice clothes from Boston, which was given to them from wealthy and more fortunate people whom they worked for. Therefore, they never knew the source of the clothes we wore. This, I think, is one reason for their jealousy, and God blessed us to have a lot of talent, even though we had a hard life. I think that coming from a large family and not having everything handed to you, so to speak, helps you to appreciate things more. If we got the finer things in life, we had to work hard, maybe twice as hard, as people do today.

I remember that even though we went to church and believed, we were also picked on there as well. I sang in the church choir. During this time, my dad was out of work due to being disabled from rheumatoid arthritis and was waiting to receive his disability compensation. The choir was collecting money from the congregation each Sunday to finance the new choir robes for us. Since my dad was not working, my aunt and uncle would put money in for me each Sunday (the money was from the people anyway), but those who could afford to give certain individual amounts each Sunday could. When the church had collected enough money for the purchase, the president and treasurer ordered the robes.

We met for choir practice on Saturday before we were to sing the next day in our new robes. After practice, everyone was asked to stay late to give out the robes. Little did they know that during practice, I had overheard the president telling her friend that she had ordered everyone's robe but mine. They thought that they would belittle me and show me up, perhaps embarrass me (this is the devil in the church now)! Ha, ha, ha. I showed them because after practice, I went home as if nothing was happening. I had done nothing to them to be treated this way. The choir director of our choir should have never allowed this to happen. He should have confronted them about this. This made me sad, but I could not let them know how I really felt.

The next day (Sunday), they expected me to sing without a robe. I fooled them again, I didn't sing with the choir; instead, I sat on the front seat in the church to show the congregation what they had done to me. Ha! Ha! I showed them up. Their plan had backfired. The preacher told them that they were wrong to do this and that they should come to me and beg pardon. I heard that they had said that "they would die and go to hell before they beg pardon." They never did until this day. Remember what I said earlier in this book, you reap what you sow? Well, I don't like to pass judgment, but one of the persons involved has had a terrible life experience with her husband and loved ones and more. She comes to me now and just hugs me. See, like they say, let the old rabbit set. I think she has guilt still in her heart, and it is eating at her by doing this to me. She comes to me and hug me. I hug her back as if she had never done anything to me, meanwhile I know God is working in my favor.

Along that same line, this same person and her brothers would destroy my mom's hats while she would sing in the church choir. We knew who was doing this. She thought we didn't know. My mom would say, "The person who continues to do this might lose their hand one of these days." Sure enough, she lost some of her fingers. They were cut off where she was working, to our surprise. I would love to tell her that this is what my mom had said would happen to her. Also, my dad and her dad worked at the same factory. Dad would say that he put his lunch in the same cubby, and her dad would put hot sauce and other unbelievable stuff in his sandwiches. I have often thought about taking her on public television and confronting her.

Betrayal (Clark)

It was 1968, I was in my second year of college and was an average ambitious young person. Actually, I had always wanted to entertain. I had always dreamed of and wished for a handsome man to sweep me off my feet. During weekends and spring breaks, I would go with my friend to her hometown, a place where there were sharecroppers and where people would hop from house to house. They sold quick drinks, and you would look in the comic paper section and find the quick lottery number you had played. I had been going home for quite some time with my friend and had met lots of guys. You could say, I had my personal pick.

I was young (nineteen years old) and had just started

to know what dating was all about. I was singing on stage in this nightclub, where my friends' brothers were performing. I had always wanted to sing and entertain on stage. Lucky for me, yahoo, I got my chance. Everyone was dancing and having a great time. We were singing "Why Not Tonight?" I had gotten halfway through the song when this tall, handsome guy walked middle ways the floor and threw kisses and extended his hand for me to come down off the stage. He was so good-looking, clean cut with curly hair, and dressed in black and white. He looked like Tony Curtis (who could resist that?). Tony Curtis was his idol, I found out later. He swept me off my feet instantly. I know I shouldn't have, but I came off that stage! We spent the rest of the evening getting acquainted and socializing.

From that time on, he and I started to converse and talk about when we could see each other again. I had met handsome men on occasions, but *no one* like this one. Several days later, he came to pick me up for our first date. He was really a clean freak—white shoes, white shirt, black pants, and black windbreaker. Those Tony Curtis curls and clean hair cut just made me melt. His name was Clark. He had the walk, the talk and everything in between.

I would stay with my friend and her family several days,

and he would come to see me. Afterward, I had to go back to school, and the party was over. I was sad because I knew it would be a while before I would see him again. After going back to school and receiving phone calls every day, I knew that he cared a lot for me. I cared a lot for him also. I thought this must be my Don Juan. I loved it.

Several months passed before the school year was over, and I had to go back to my hometown. After not hearing from Clark, my parents didn't have a phone, I wondered if he still had me in his heart. I certainly had him in mine.

Clark did not know where I lived and had never heard of the town of Billings. Unexpectedly, he showed up at my parent's house. He had caught the Greyhound Bus and had come to the little city part of town, questioned some people as to where my family lived, and had gotten a ride for about ten to fifteen miles to see me. Now I knew this man must have seen something in me or had feelings for me.

Clark stayed several days, and after meeting my family, he seemed to like them very much. He stayed at my aunt's house out of respect because we weren't married to each other. My aunt lived by herself and had to protect what she owned, and she was on up in age. My aunt said she told him not to play the TV all night and to observe some other rules she had. She later told me, "He might try to kill you." He must have really made my aunt angry. Sure enough, in the end, he did try to kill me. I never thought this would ever happen. I will attempt to explain to you later in my story how he tried to kill me. Unfortunately, my aunt didn't live long enough for me to tell her that she was right.

After Clark returned home, he decided that we were too far away from each other to maintain our relationship. We decided to move together. He would walk the street with me and serenade me on street corners, kissing me and all (like a fairy tale). I just loved this man! As we got to know each other more, his mom told me about how his dad would bolt the windows with nails while he went to work in the fields to keep her from encountering some of the workers. We got close even though I would go to work for two shifts (tours) per day most of the time. We decided to get married, so we went across the state line and got married the next day. Now, I said to myself, I finally got him hooked, whoo-hoo! I was really in love with this man. I knew he loved me too; I never thought anything would ruin our relationship. We went places, such as concerts, dances, fairs, movies, and ball games. Life was good.

Something strange happened in which I never could

understand. Clark mentioned that his brother had a girlfriend and a wife, and he couldn't decide which one he wanted to be with, so he killed his girlfriend and didn't receive any jail time for it. This to me was unbelievable. Another thing was that he said he had always asked God to let him live until he was thirty-two years of age. I don't think he really knew that being thirty-two was still young. Why? It was amazing to me or ironic, I'm not sure which. It's very strange. Later, I will explain how significant these two events are in my story.

We lived happy for several years after we married, until one day, Clark came home from work and accused me of having a boyfriend. He said, "I am trying to find out what I'm working for!" Then he started kicking and shoving me around, trying to make me get in the car. He started hitting me in the nose, which caused my nose to bleed. Meanwhile I was fighting him back and screaming, "Leave me alone!" I was wearing a white pants suit, and by the time he had finished hitting me, the pant suit was bloody from top to bottom. He said, "My friend told me at work today that you have a boyfriend, and you are going with me to prove it" (he meant to his friend's house). I said, "I don't have a boyfriend and you can't prove anything." Also, I was at work most of the time, and if I had one, how would I ever have time to see him? I said, "You are the one running around on me. You're constantly dressing up, singing, and whistling while in the shower, so what can that mean?" I worked in telephone communications, and most of the time, I worked two tours per day.

I remember that the weekend before he did this, we had gone clubbing with our friend and his wife. While there, he had asked this man (whom I didn't know) to dance with me. He said, "Dance with my wife." We sat there a while and had a few drinks. In about an hour, two women walked in. Immediately, Clark got up to get a chair for them. I knew that this was one of his close girlfriends. About a month later, we would get our mail at the hotel lobby where we were living at this time. He meant to get rid of this letter before he came back with the mail, but he forgot. I asked him, "Who is this letter from?" He said nothing and tore the letter up quickly and threw it in the garbage. Immediately, I grabbed the garbage can and went running into the bathroom and locked the door. During this time, I put the card back together. This was how I found out who it was from. It was from a lady named Emily, whom he had been seeing. In the next day or so, I found out where she lived and got her phone number. I called her and asked her to discontinue seeing him because he was my husband. He found out and said, "She will never call me again." I said to myself, "Bet I beat you to the punch." Then I said, "Why do you care, I am your wife, not her." That was really something to say to me (his wife) (heartbreaking). What did he think about me? Did he care or even love me now? After that, I always knew when Clark was going whore hopping because he would sing or whistle love songs in the shower. Usually, he would sing a song by Bobby Goldsboro, whose lyrics say, "Honey I miss you and I'm being good; I'd love to be with you if only I could."

About a month prior to this happening, he accused me of liking his brother, who was living with us, and he knocked me off the edge of our porch. In the process, I called the police, and they told me to take out a warrant for him. I didn't though because I had thought I would never have any more problems with him doing this again.

Clark would invite students who were attending college from his hometown to our house (thinking I was stupid, I guess) and then take them home and take several hours to return home when it would only take ten minutes.

There was a time when another one of our friends

(husband and wife) were visiting us. Her husband and him were supposed to be attending a game and was to pick us up later at our friend's house. Well, later never came. So we decided to go check on them at my house. The two of them were asleep and could not be awakened. We had to break the glass in the door to get in. Afterward (the next day), I realized that my husband had changed clothes. I checked the clothes hamper, and there was his shirt and pants in the bottom of it. The shirt was bloody on the front from top to bottom. I wonder if he had been going with his friend, a man, or some woman on her period? Now this had begun to get very questionable and creepy. My heart was hurt, and I was losing trust in the man I once loved.

After the incident about him proving that I had a boyfriend, Clark went out and bought a shotgun. I really got upset. Later, he went and bought me a box of candy (I guess to soothe me). He gave me the safety for the gun, but I could never put it on. He also bought a shovel (to bury me). Now I was beginning to get real shaky and nervous, but I couldn't let him know.

One evening after work a few weeks after this, Clark threw my clothes and shoes in the backyard (in the city limits), poured gas on them, and set them on fire; and then he sat there watching them burn. This was when I really got upset. I said to myself, *He has bought this gun and shovel and told me about his brother having a girlfriend and wife and couldn't decide what to do, so he killed his girlfriend and didn't get a day for it.* So you know just what Clark was planning to do to me. After he burned my clothes, several weeks later, we went to the Bahamas on vacation. I had to go out and buy new clothes to go on vacation. I was so disgusted and frightened that I was afraid to tell his family or mine. By this time, it had gotten so that I didn't get very much sleep. Who could I confide in? I didn't want my parents or anyone to know that this was happening to me.

Clark was talking to me one day because I could see by now that he really wasn't the loving man that I had expected him to be. He was trying to go with my little sister. We went out one night, my three sisters, me, and him. He asked her (my little sister) for a dance, and as we looked around, he was kissing her. My sister blurted out, "Look ya'll, he is kissing her." Also, he pretended to be helping her learn how to drive and was going with her. (I don't know why she never said anything to me about this.) He also would ask her to go to the store with him. They stayed much too long. At this time, I never expected anything because I trusted him and her. After all this had happened, I began to get upset.

Later, I had gotten pregnant and unfortunately had a miscarriage. Clark came to the hospital to see me and brought another woman with him, pretending that she wanted to see me. I didn't want to see her because I knew why she was with him. I was so disgruntled. I cried and asked God to help me. I knew his day was coming; every dog has his day. This was a very miserable time for me. I don't really know how I got through it.

Maybe I was so in love with Clark until I was blinded or maybe afraid, I didn't know what it was. Young and dumb, I guess. If I had known what type of man he was, I would have stayed up on the stage that night and continued singing, "Why did I come down tonight?" (LOL)

After all the stuff he had done to me, he would have the nerve to get jealous when he would drop me off at work. The guys would whistle at me (at that time, I was slim with hips and a small waistline). He would get so jealous. This was him showing his guilt for what he was doing to me. He wanted to have his cake and eat it too. Clark would be so angry with the guys that he would attempt to turn around, but instead he sped away. Little did he know that several of the guys had asked me for a date, but I refused. I was married, and two wrongs don't make a right.

One time while I was working, an old college friend came to see me. She didn't know that I had to work, so she waited on me at our house. She called me at work in a little while, crying. She said that he was trying to rape her while she waited on me to get off work. What a dog! He had told a friend that he was going to get all the pussy that he could before he died. Sadly, Clark thought he was the best when it came to sex. Well, he was a good lover. He said, "When I die, I want you to pickle my penis, so you can have it forever." Clark liked this song, "Honey, I miss you and I'm being good. I'd love to be with you if only I could," by Bobby Goldsboro. He also said that when he died, he wanted me to plant a tree on his grave. I don't know what the tree symbolized.

Several months went by, and one day, we were talking. Clark was still making accusations that I had a boyfriend. His mom came to visit us. Instead of staying home and entertaining her, he used this time to go dating. Here he was, singing in the shower again. He would always drink bourbon on a regular basis. He called it his bor-burn.

Because I was a country girl. I didn't know anything

about catching bugs (crabs, bed bugs, etc.). Well, while at work one day, I started to itch below. I couldn't sit still. I had to leave my work space and go use the bathroom. I was almost dancing in my chair, like popcorn; they were biting on me so much. I discovered later that I had crabs. He had given them to me (disgusting). It was terrible. I guess he caught them from some of his bitches. After going through all of this, I decided that this couldn't be what love is!

Three to four months passed. Thank God I had just gotten my driver's license. A few weeks later, he said to me, "If you ever leave me, I am going up to your mom and dad's house and kill the whole family, even if it takes me a month. I will lay in the woods and knock them off until I get them all. I will kill the first one of your little sisters that I see in the yard." My heart sank, I didn't know whether to scream, cry, or what to do.

The Dream

Two nights before Clark started mistreating me, I had this dream. Clark was in the pool room shooting pool, a favorite pastime of his, along with my uncle and my brother. The mistreatment started when I had this big dream about the devil with huge feet, and in this dream, there was a devil more than six feet tall roaming and r-o-a-r-ing loudly about in the pool room with huge feet resembling a clown's feet.

The dream was that the devil and my then first husband, Clark, was in the pool room. The devil with great big feet and horns was walking around, roaming around them in this pool room. At that time, I felt that this was an omen for Clark to stop drinking, running around, and whore hopping, and for my uncle to straighten up and stop some of the drinking and get right with God. This was the devil after them, and they needed to be aware of what they were doing wrong.

I was reminded that my uncle used to get drunk and wallow all over the place and go to sleep on the ground after he had gotten paid each week and had gone to the house where his so-called girlfriend was. Someone would take his money after he had gotten drunk. He loved to drink, and when this would happen, he would mix up all sorts of food like cabbage and pinto beans with lots and lots of onions. Boy would his breath smell from the bootleg (corn liquor) in which he drank earlier. This would happen every week. I remember him lying on the ground one Sunday afternoon after getting drunk, and the dogs went up to him while he slept and smelled his mouth and lick him. We really got a laugh out of that.

Well, to my surprise, within three months' time after this having this dream, my husband was dead. My uncle died with D-Tees because of drinking his corn liquor. I remember my uncle being a nice, good, fun-loving person, who was very talented. He could make most anything carving; he would whittle away at wood and make many odd things. He once made his own bed with a chest to match and was very handy with carving out statues just using his imagination. He once whittled some cats and an old lady sitting in a rocking chair. Both pieces were amazing.

Shortly after that, my sister was killed by her husband in cold blood at a reception; instead of my brother, who was in the dream in the pool room.

I told Clark about this dream and about my brother. I explained to him that they were in this pool room and about this devil, but he ignored me. Guess he had his mind made up as to what he was going to do.

Next in line after my dream was what happened to me.

Well, two nights later, Clark got the shotgun and loaded it. I was really upset and frightened. I was hollering, "Please, please don't kill me!" He held the gun in one hand, got a big glass of bourbon, and said, "You drink it." I gulped the bourbon down as he instructed me. It burned my throat. Apparently, I didn't get intoxicated though; I guess I was too afraid to. Afterward, I stood there crying and sobbing and really in shock. Then he took his belt off and beat me with the buckle on my backside until I couldn't sit down. My buttock was black. I was numb unable to move. Then he got the scissors (still with the gun) in hand and cut my hair off in all kinds of lengths. He said, "I dare you not to go to work Monday." I was crying and sobbing and really afraid to move, not knowing what he might do next. I had to figure what my strategy was. I could not take any more of this; I had to do something!

Meanwhile, I guess Clark got tired. Eventually, he said angrily, "We need to go to bed." I was crying and hollering and begging him not to kill me! We somehow went to bed. I couldn't sleep. He cut the lights off and put the gun on the kitchen table, still loaded. I started to go and get it and kill him in his sleep, but I thought, *Even though he has done all this to you, you still don't have the nerve to do it.* (I guess it wasn't God's will.) My mom, dad, and family members didn't know that this was happening. I thought that I would rather be dead myself than my whole family. I did not deserve this, nor did any of my family members. And I had no way to tell them except writing them or calling the nosey neighbor, who live about a quarter of a mile away.

After a while, Clark was snoring loudly and had his leg wrapped over me so he could feel me move. I was lying there, heart pounding, thinking about how I would manage to get away safely. I eased up in the dark, eased his leg off me, and scrammed around (seeing by the moonlight shining through the window) to put my shorts and a blouse on (no underclothes or shoes). I found the key in the dark and my pocketbook. I quietly eased into the kitchen, by the gun on the table, and opened the back door. The dog was at the door. I just knew that he would bark and awaken him. The dog never made any noise. I left the back door wide open with him still asleep. Nervous and panicky, I got in the car and sped away. I went to the police station to take out a warrant. I told them what had happened and what Clark had said he would do if I left him. They said if I did take out a warrant, then he would certainly do what he had promised to do. So I told them I was getting out of town, my man and I were done. If something happened, at least the police would know what to tell my family. I drove for about twenty to thirty miles to Gibson until 2:00 a.m. I parked the car on a back street in Redburn. I thought that since he cared so much about our car (Clark felt that the car was important to his lifestyle with women), if I took the car to my parent's house, he would surely know where I was. Therefore, I called one of my work partners and explained to him what had happened and that I was going to park my car on a back street and catch a taxi to Billings. At that time, I had to pay $35—all that I had. (I wasn't worried because I was saving my life.) Whew! Thank God.

After getting to my parents' house, I told the family what had happened. They could see my hair all cut in splotches and that I was terrified. About ten Sunday morning, here comes a car from out of state. It was his work boss bringing him to find me. My dad told him that he hadn't seen or heard from me. I was hiding, peeping out the window where he couldn't see me. After riding close by the house where he thought he could see good enough, he went back to Gibson. He said to my father in a loud voice, "I'll be back."

Meanwhile, we went to the police station in Merrysville and Billings to get a warrant to keep him from returning. They told us that if we didn't see him with a weapon, then they couldn't issue us a warrant.

Around dusk, here comes a taxi with out-of-state tags on it. It was him returning. My dad had been sitting on the porch with a shotgun across his lap, waiting for him because he said he would return. We had been afraid all day long because we did not know where he was or when he would return. Clark got out of the taxi with the shotgun under two suitcoats. He started toward our house, walking swiftly on the back of his loafers. (He was wearing white loafers because he loved black and white clothes and looked good in them.) He came up on the porch, so I was told. I could hear him, but I was still in hiding in the back room. He knocked my mom aside with the shotgun. My mom pleaded with him to put the gun away, saying, "Clark, I don't want any trouble." He then forced my dad to go into the house, knocked the porch light out, and told my dad not to pick up anything. He said, "I am giving you ten minutes, nine minutes, eight minutes, and so on to get my wife." My dad didn't make any attempts to get me, so he stepped back and proceeded to cock the shotgun to kill my dad. Little did he know, my dad had a pistol in his side pocket, waiting. He was prepared because he said he would be back. My dad pulled it out and shot him in the forehead before he could do him. He fell on the floor on top, the gun breathing hard. As he lay there bleeding profusely, my mind went blank. I was screaming, "Why, why, why?" My sister was in the back room with a friend. She heard the shot and shouted, "Lord, have mercy!"

Clark never regained consciousness. When the police arrived, one policeman had to hold his hand and one on the trigger to keep the gun from firing. This was how close he came to killing my dad. I hate that my dad had to do this, but I believe it was a clear matter of self-defense.

He was taken to the hospital and died at sunrise. The significance of this was that he named our dog Sunrise and he died at sunrise, and he said he had asked God to let him live until he was thirty-two, and he was thirty-two years old.

For months after this happened to me, I would be driving along the highway and I would see animals and different things jumping out of the bushes in front of me. My momma would have to ride with me and keep me company. Fortunately, with the help of God and my mother constantly talking to me and praying, I did not have to go see a psychiatrist. However, I still have a lot of anxiety out of the ordeal I had been through. This situation could easily cause a person to have mental issues.

After Clark was killed by my dad, we discovered that he had gone by my uncle's house to ask them to come with him to look for me, but they refused. He said we were all liars and sons of bitches. Later, we discovered a note he had left on the table at our residence in Gibson. You know, his mom said, "A drunk man will die with his shoes on," and he did. She also said that his dad was so jealous over her that when his dad went to work in the tobacco fields, he would bar the windows shut them with nails until he came home. Insane jealousy. Do you call this love, jealousy, or insanity?

Deception (Tom)

After Clark's death, I moved back home to Billings and found a job in Merryville. Eventually, I got back into communications. Of course, I was sad and heartbroken, but life went on. After two years, I got involved with my second husband because my mom envisioned that he was going to be good for me. He, too, was very handsome. He was a PK. You know, a preacher's kid. His name was Tom. Since I had gone through with so much with my first husband, my mom told me that God had shown her a man for me and the location as to where he lived (in a dream). Sure enough, this location was exactly where God showed her.

I met Tom at a nightclub, and we hit it off like we had known each other for some time. Tom was a good, sentimental person who would cry at the drop of a hat, but he really wasn't my type. I never really saw him as a possible spouse. We would go out on weekends with his cousin, her husband, and my sisters. (They say we sisters stuck together and looked out for each other. If you mess with one, you had trouble from all.) While I worked, Tom ran around with my cousins and his so-called friends. He would pretend that he always loved me and try to do work, etc., to impress me when he was really fronting his feelings.

My cousin often said, "If Tom would only treat you right, everything would be alright." I wondered why she was saying that. He was running around with her sons. She knew what he was doing; I was the last to know. Every weekend, he would ride around with his friends while I would be at work; when I got off, he would be all intoxicated. I wondered why I always meet these types of men and prayed that God would send me someone different. Tom and I would take trips to the beach with his family and go out on fishing boats. I loved the social activity.

About a year later, Tom and I got married. He was a mill worker, and I was still working in communications at a local telephone company. I would transport him to work because he lost his driver's license due to alcohol addiction. Tom blamed me because he came looking for me (he didn't have to since I was a little late arriving home after work). He got caught driving under the influence and, as a result, lost his driving privileges.

Before Tom and I were married, I used to make some of his clothes, and we would play match game. I was always peticular about my clothes and how my close friends looked. We were close, or so I thought, and he loved the clothes and the attention I gave him. I used to drop him off to stay at his mom's while I worked two tours per day at times.

When Tom went to work, I was packing him two lunches (supposedly for him alone), one for his break and one for his lunch. I always wondered how he ate all this food.

To my surprise, one day I received a letter at work, saying, "You don't deserve to be treated this way. Your husband has a woman pregnant (big as a cow) and is feeding her every day, and you know who she is. Well, I didn't know right away, but I quickly found out. My sister said she wondered why he was packing so much lunch.

I was told that while I was dropping Tom off at his mom's, she was picking him up, and that I would almost run into her in the process. After that, when I would go to his mom's house (preacher's wife) (Mom and Dad lived beside each other in separate houses), they called him the Preacher and laughed about it; there would be a picture of a little child on the mantle. They jokingly called him Sugar. Little did I know that this was the child my husband fathered and the woman that Tom was feeding with the extra lunch he took every day. She was Little Sugar's mother (hurtful). I was the last to know.

The Preacher would come to have lunch with us on occasions and put his corn liquor bottle down beside his feet and say, "Don't tell anybody about it." Little did he know that God knew what he was doing. Then he would occasionally go with us on trips, and when we would stop for gas, he would say, "Off again, on again, gone again, flanagan." He was kind of comical, but I thought he could not be an example for others when he was doing the things he did. It was not for me to judge.

In addition, while I was at work, Tom tried to have sex with an older sister of mine, telling her that he had been giving her cigarettes and acted as if she owed him sex because of it. One day I was sick in bed and something told me to go into the kitchen. Tom was sitting talking to several of my younger sisters and was feeling on the legs of one of them. Enough with this mess from my men, I told him I would beat the crap out of him if he didn't stop and report him to authorities, because they were minors. He had constantly told me that he had something to tell me, but never could tell me. This little Sugar was what he was trying to tell me, his little dirty secret. My sister and I went to his workplace to give the lady a kind surprise. When they came out after work, I lounged out of the car. I said (with a knife in my hand), "Since you have been sneaking around with my husband, I came to get you." She ran and got in the car with one of her friends and left her car. The next day, I was told that her mom came there, waiting on me and my sister with a gun. She could run with my husband but wasn't woman enough to defend her actions.

After having dealt with this, I was literally destroyed. I was so devastated that I decided to take Tom to the woman that he had been seeing behind my back. To his amazement, I found out where she lived, and one snowy day, when he had been drinking, he fell asleep in the car. When he woke up, I had arrived at her door. I told her "Here he is, I don't want him anymore." I said to her, "Since you have been sneaking around with my husband, you can have him." Tom would not get out of the car. He had to realize that after I had gone through all the trauma with my first husband, I didn't need any more of this drama. How much more could I stand? Here again, God was with the plan, still making me stronger for some reason.

Accidents

During the time that I was with Clark, we would often travel. Once when we were going to my mom's house, a driver stopped abruptly in front of us, causing us to get hit in the back and causing me to get a slight concussion. Clark just sat there like nothing had happened because he wasn't hurt and because he had been drinking. He knew not to speak up in our defense, leaving me injured and having to defend myself.

While I was with Tom, we decided to go out for the evening with my sister and her boyfriend. Tom told my sister's friend to drive. Little did I know that he did not have a driver's license. So while traveling, it had been raining, and the road was still wet. Tom told his cousin to pass my sister and her friend, who we were following. When he proceeded to accelerate, the car spun around in the roadway and hit the ditch, just missing a tree. I was thrown into the windshield, and my arm was broken. That was terrifying and really shook me up. Everyone got out of the car, but me. I was sitting there wondering why I couldn't move. My arm had been broken away from my torso. I had to be rushed to the hospital and put into traction for a month. Pins were put in and weights applied to pull my arm back in place. No partying for us, especially me. I lay in the hospital for weeks. Pins ran through my elbow with weights, and my arm sat upward for at least a month. I got out of the hospital, and I had numbness and my arm had grown in the bent shape that they had put it in. So I couldn't extend my arm without the doctor pulling on it. The doctor said that the grooves my nerves fit into were destroyed, so he had to install psylastic to make more grooves to fit my nerves. Why me? The doctor would try to pull my arm out, and I would scream before he applied this feature. I'm thankful that this could happen. It took away all the misery and numbness. I will have this thing in my arm for a lifetime now. Why me, Lord? It had to be me. All of what I had to go through has made me a stronger person.

During the next few years, I met husband number 3, even though Tom and I were not separated legally yet.

Love (Ethan)

While I stopped by this restaurant after work, this handsome, tall gentleman walked in (in a blue leisure suit) and sat down. I said to myself, *Huh, what a nice-looking man, looks like Clark Gable.* Guess I might have been staring because after a while, he sent a message to me by the waitress, asking me to have a drink. I accepted. Soon we were talking and getting to know each other better.

Later, I discovered that I knew this man. We had been passing by him on Sunday mornings years before. He was going to his church and me to mine. He was tall and handsome, and at that time, it looked as if his head was touching the top of the car. The younger girls, about the age of sixteen, would say on Sunday after church, they would go to his church later to see that good-looking man, Ethan.

Little did I know that this was the same man that I would meet so many years later. God had to be looking out for me after all my misfortunes. My first husband tried to kill me, as I mentioned, and my second husband ran out on me and impregnated another woman.

Well, we decided to start seeing each other. I would take my second husband to work, and we would meet. I had no intentions of going out on my second husband, but I was so upset after all he had done to me that I had to find some peace of mind. Our friends would invite us to cookouts, etc., at their houses, and we would just enjoy being with each other.

Several weeks passed, and I would have to pick Tom up. Ethan said, "Take my car, my new car with out-of-state tags." He didn't know me, but must have seen something in me to trust me. When I drove up at Tom's workplace, he asked, "Whose car is this?" I said, "It's my long-lost cousin from Berkville," whom he had never met.

As time went by, Tom and I would get together with Ethan, and they would play cards and so on. Then we would go out to restaurants together. While at the restaurant,

Tom would be intoxicated and cram his jaws with food. He looked like a squirrel with nut in his jaws, perhaps a squirrel packing away for the winter. Ethan whispered to me and said, "Take that disgusting nutcase home." Tom was still thinking that Ethan was my long-lost cousin. My lost cousin had a friend whom he would see and socialize with before he met me. She said she was pregnant by Ethan. Well, Ethan had been out of town for so many years, and she was still married. Her husband was an alcoholic and would stay intoxicated all the time. I don't suppose he even knew that his wife was going out on him. Ethan and I still pretended to be cousins when the four of us would get together. Only he and I knew the true story. Ethan was supposed to be headed to Texas for a new job, but after meeting me, he changed his mind. Wow.

I had told Tom that I couldn't take anymore and that I wanted him to leave my house. I couldn't get him to leave. My brother and his wife were living with me also. While I was still working, Ethan wanted me to be with him, but I told him that I had obligations and could not leave my job. Ethan borrowed $3,000 so that I could pay off my bills. Afterward, I packed up, and Ethan and I moved to New England and left Tom there.

Several months passed, when Ethan told me he had to get his things in order and wouldn't tell me what he had to do (I thought we had broken up), and I guess I really didn't know where things stood with us. Tom came to New England on the bus and said he came to get me. I went back home with him for about a week. To my surprise, Ethan came to get me and explained what had happened. I was so elated. I guess that's the way love is. I was so very, very happy and pleased that he had come to retrieve his soulmate (me). I loved every minute of it. My mother told him that he would take me back to the city and make a prostitute out of me. He said, "I will prove her wrong." And he did. Later, my mom said that he was the best son-in-law she had ever had. Ethan would sing to me regularly and serenade me. The favorite song he would sing is "Such a fine brown frame. Honey, won't you tell me your name. You look sweet to me and all I can see is my fine brown frame." That gave me the most peaceful feeling I have ever had.

We worked things out and got back together. I finally decided that this was my new life. Ethan asked me to move with him in my hometown. I accepted. I knew this was my chance for happiness. After about a year, Ethan and I got married and had our first child, a beautiful baby girl. She was a living doll. When we traveled, sometimes it would be raining, and she would press her little nose against the window and people would laugh. She would laugh also.

I knew that Ethan was a go-getter. He had worked as a construction worker, a baker's helper, a milkman, ride operator for the carnival, a lift truck operator, and an eighteen-wheeler trucker. He was a warehouseman, served in the navy, and was a postman. He never let anything stop him. He brought me several cars, and to him, nothing was ever too good for me. He took care of me as no other man had ever done. He took me to New York and bought me the best food, clothes, and accessories money could buy. We traveled a lot from New York to Virginia and throughout the United States.

I knew I had finally found a stable life and someone who really loved and cared for me. We did everything together. We traveled all over the country. He took me everywhere. Several years passed, and we had a second child, a beautiful baby boy, another living doll.

Ethan began to get sick. He had serious problems. Through it all, he never allowed anything to stop him. But I have learned that life is not easy and that God will allow you to go through tough times to make you stronger.

Every summer, we would pack up after the kids got out of school and take a month to travel across country. We got a travel trailer and would drive several hundred miles per day, and as we saw attractions nearby, we would stay a day or so to sightsee and enjoy. One summer while traveling, I happened to look at the map, and in very fine print, it said, "No gas for 100 miles." I told Ethan. He said, "We will never make it." We were in Utah on our way to California. When he said that, my heart sank. Ethan immediately tried to flag down someone in order to catch a ride. We had no idea how far and how long it would take. Suddenly, some guys driving a motor home with California license plates stopped and scooped him up. I thought, *Here I am with these two small children, and I am out here in the middle of no man's land.* I immediately took the license plate down because he may not return. He was riding with total strangers, and at that time, there were no cell phones, etc. After he left, I was out there alone, and I could barely see cars in the distance; they looked like little matchboxes. I was really afraid! So at that time, we would always travel with our personal security. I said to myself if any predator came along, I was ready for them. Still, I was so afraid because I didn't know if he would return or what time.

Finally, at about dusk, here he comes with $10 worth of gas and had to pay $100 for it (that included the mileage). By that time, I had gotten a little intoxicated because I was so afraid I had to calm my nerves. Ethan said, "What have you gotten into?" I said, "The calming juice." LOL. Well, everything went well; he was back, and we could travel a little further. We would normally travel about 200 to 300 miles per day, and if we saw any attractions, we would settle there for several days. Fortunately, we traveled back to where he had purchased the gas and camped out there for the night. I said to Ethan, "From now on, when we get down to one-half a tank of gas, we are going to fill up again."

Our family went from here to California, Canada, and Mexico. I delighted in our travels and learned a lot. If I had never met my handsome soulmate, I probably would have been still sitting in the same place. I feel that after all the deceptions and heartaches, God sent me this man so that I could be happy again and for the rest of my life. After everything I went through with Clark and Tom, I found true love with my Clark Gable (Ethan) that lasted his lifetime.

Before he died, he told me that he had a dream. In this

dream, he saw me standing in the middle of a rose garden, and as he watched, I got smaller and farther and farther away from him. He told me that he loved me and would see me someday. It was an omen from God showing me that he was going to die. He had gotten really sick and was in a coma-like state several times, but each time, he would bounce back. When he passed, I could not come to terms with his being gone for good. He said he told his nurses about the dream, and they all said, "What a love story!" Ethan did pass away.

In Conclusion

Out of all the disappointments that I have had in my life, God has blessed me. They say the good will overcome the bad. I often wonder about different things that have happened in my life, and I attribute it to my sheltered upbringing. Growing up in a family of sixteen taught me a lot of things. However, the only thing I wish is that we had experienced more of learning about people and the way they are. I guess you would say dealing with people in everyday life. We didn't have a chance to see just how different people react and handle situations. We grew up in the country and dealt with people mainly through church and school. The people we dealt with were also country. We never experienced street people or, should I say, city people and their type of life. We always thought that everyone was nice and honest and truthful. I had no idea that people would be deceitful or lie to your face or do you bodily harm. We were never taught about the bad things in life, nor did we know what Mother meant when she said something might happen sometimes in childlike terms. I have had to learn the hard way. I did learn a lot too late.

It is true that experience is the best teacher. My first-hand situations taught me about trust, or the lack thereof, and deception and lies outright in the face. Love is used lightly and expressed from the mouth, but not the heart. Living in the moment is very real for some people. Take what you want; do not worry about anyone else or their feelings. If your heart gets broken, you are weak and shame on you. Learn to live with it and toughen up. Only the strong survive. If at any time in your life you find true love, good for you. By all means, cherish it.

Lightning Source UK Ltd.
Milton Keynes UK
UKHW011900200921
390927UK00008B/437/J